Everybody's Favorite Series No. 3

Trade Mark

Piano Pieces for Children

FOREWORD *The compositions in* Children's Piano Pieces *have been carefully and progressively graded. Many are presented in new and interesting arrangements. Both educational and recreational values have been considered by the editor, Maxwell Eckstein, in the preparation of this work.*

The scope of the material is broad and thorough. It ranges from the works of the great masters to the folk tunes and dances of many lands, encompassing grades one through four.

The success of Children's Piano Pieces, *Number 3 in the popular* Everybody's Favorite Series, *is apparent. For years this publication has been a "best-seller". It is so because of the basic material presented as well as the means of presentation. If you enjoy our publication our satisfaction is doubled.* **THE PUBLISHER**

Maxwell Eckstein, Editor

Copyright © 1934 Renewed 1951 by Amsco Music Publishing Company,
A Division of Music Sales Corporation, New York
All Rights Reserved

International Standard Book Number: 0.8256.2003.1

Exclusive Distributors:
Music Sales Corporation
24 East 22nd Street, New York, New York 10010 USA
Music Sales Limited
8/9 Frith Street, London W1V 5TZ England
Music Sales Pty. Limited
27 Clarendon Street, Artarmon, Sydney NSW 2064 Australia

Printed and bound in the United States of America by
Vicks Lithograph and Printing Corporation

PIANO PIECES FOR CHILDREN
COMPOSER'S INDEX

BACH
GAVOTTE — 94
GAVOTTE IN D — 18
GAVOTTE IN G — 82
MUSETTE — 27
PRELUDE No. 1 IN C — 148

BAUMFELDER
PEASANT DANCE — 36

BAYLY
LONG, LONG AGO — 12

BEETHOVEN
ANDANTE — 112
ECOSSAISES — 180
FUR ELISE — 73
GERTRUDE'S DREAM WALTZ — 52
MINUET IN G — 100
TURKISH MARCH — 14

BEHR
CAMP OF THE GYPSIES — 136
FRENCH CHILD'S SONG — 4
IN MAY — 5

BISHOP
HOME SWEET HOME — 16

BOHM
FOUNTAIN, THE — 83

BRAGA
ANGEL'S SERENADE — 79

BRAHMS
CRADLE SONG — 20
HUNGARIAN DANCE — 108
WALTZ IN A FLAT — 122

BURGMULLER
ARABESQUE — 39

CAREY
AMERICA — 63

CHAMINADE
SCARF DANCE — 141

CHOPIN
FUNERAL MARCH — 42
MAZURKA IN B FLAT — 126
PRELUDE OP. 28 No. 7 — 95
PRELUDE OP. 28 No. 20 — 95

CLEMENTI
SONATINA — 30

DAQUIN
LE COUCOU — 150

DELIBES
VALSE LENTE (COPPELIA) — 109

DURAND
CHACONNE — 164

DVORAK
HUMORESQUE — 160

ELLMENREICH
SPINNING SONG — 90

FLOTOW
LAST ROSE OF SUMMER — 17

FOSTER
KENTUCKY HOME — 116
OLD BLACK JOE — 117
SWANEE RIVER — 116

GODARD
BERCEUSE (JOCELYN) — 71

GOUNOD
FAUST WALTZ — 40

GRIEG
ALBUMLEAF — 96
GRANDMOTHER'S MINUET — 104

GRUBER
SILENT NIGHT — 12

GURLITT
THE FAIR — 10

HANDEL
LARGO — 81

HARRISON
IN THE GLOAMING — 29

HAYDN
ANDANTE (SURPRISE SYMPHONY) — 7

HELLER
AVALANCHE — 24
CURIOUS STORY — 76

LANGE
IN RANK AND FILE — 56

LEHAR
MERRY WIDOW WALTZ — 134

LICHNER
AT HOME — 50
GIPSY DANCE — 118
ON THE MEADOW — 97
TULIP — 43

MARGIS
VALSE BLEUE — 128

MASSENET
ARAGONAISE — 156
ELEGIE — 154

MENDELSSOHN
CONSOLATION — 66
SPRING SONG — 64
VENETIAN BOAT SONG No. 2 — 124

MOLLOY
LOVE'S OLD SWEET SONG — 31

MOZART
MINUET (DON JUAN) — 15

OESTEN
DOLL'S DREAM — 67

OFFENBACH
BARCAROLLE (TALES OF HOFFMAN) — 88

PIECZONKA
TARANTELLA — 173

POLDINI
WALTZING DOLL — 168

RIMSKY-KORSAKOFF
SONG OF INDIA — 144

RUBINSTEIN
MELODY IN F — 28

SAINT-SAENS
THE SWAN — 70

SCHUBERT
MOMENT MUSICAL — 92
SERENADE — 132
UNFINISHED SYMPHONY — 34

SCHUMANN
JOYOUS FARMER — 23
KNIGHT RUPERT — 86
MELODY — 7
ROMANCE — 107
SOLDIER'S MARCH — 38
TRAUMEREI — 106

SMALLWOOD
THE HAREBELL — 8

SMITH
STAR SPANGLED BANNER — 63

SPINDLER
TRUMPETER'S SERENADE — 46

STRAUSS
BEAUTIFUL BLUE DANUBE — 186

STREABOGG
FAIRY WALTZ — 32

TSCHAIKOWSKY
GERMAN SONG — 35
ITALIAN SONG — 26
WALTZ OP. 39 — 54
WALTZ OF THE FLOWERS — 113

VAN GAEL
VOICE OF THE HEART — 48

VON WEBER
CRADLE SONG — 19
OBERON — 20

YRADIER
LA PALOMA — 101

FOLK TUNES

AMERICAN
TURKEY IN THE STRAW — 22

FRENCH
AH! VOUS DIRAIS-JE-MAMAN — 6
AU CLAIR DE LA LUNE — 6

IRISH
LONDONDERRY AIR — 60

SCOTCH
AULD LANG SYNE — 19

RUSSIAN
DARK EYES — 13
VOLGA BOAT SONG — 78

VIENNESE
VIENNESE MELODY — 62

PIANO PIECES FOR CHILDREN
CONTENTS

AH! VOUS DIRAIS-JE-MAMAN	French Folk Tune	6
ALBUMLEAF	Grieg	96
AMERICA	Carey	63
ANGEL'S SERENADE	Braga	79
ANDANTE	Beethoven	112
ANDANTE (Surprise Symphony)	Haydn	7
ARABESQUE	Burgmuller	39
ARAGONAISE	Massenet	156
AT HOME	Lichner	50
AU CLAIR DE LA LUNE	French Folk Tune	6
AULD LANG SYNE	Scotch Folk Tune	19
AVALANCHE	Heller	24
BARCAROLLE (Tales of Hoffman)	Offenbach	88
BEAUTIFUL BLUE DANUBE	Strauss	186
BERCEUSE (Jocelyn)	Godard	71
CAMP OF THE GYPSIES	Behr	136
CHACONNE	Durand	164
CONSOLATION	Mendelssohn	66
CURIOUS STORY	Heller	76
CRADLE SONG	Brahms	20
CRADLE SONG	Von Weber	19
DARK EYES	Russian Folk Song	13
DOLL'S DREAM	Oesten	67
ECOSSAISES	Beethoven-Busoni	180
ELEGIE	Massenet	154
FAIR, THE	Gurlitt	10
FAIRY WALTZ	Streabogg	32
FAUST WALTZ	Gounod	40
FOUNTAIN, THE	Bohm	83
FRENCH CHILD'S SONG	Behr	4
FUR ELISE	Beethoven	73
FUNERAL MARCH	Chopin	42
GAVOTTE	Bach	94
GAVOTTE IN D	Bach	18
GAVOTTE IN G	Bach	82
GERMAN SONG	Tschaikowsky	35
GERTRUDE'S DREAM WALTZ	Beethoven	52
GIPSY DANCE	Lichner	118
GRANDMOTHER'S MINUET	Grieg	104
HAREBELL, THE	Smallwood	8
HOME SWEET HOME	Bishop	16
HUMORESQUE	Dvorak	160
HUNGARIAN DANCE	Brahms	108
IN MAY	Behr	5
IN RANK AND FILE	Lange	56
IN THE GLOAMING	Harrison	29
ITALIAN SONG	Tschaikowsky	26
JOYOUS FARMER	Schumann	23
KENTUCKY HOME	Foster	116
KNIGHT RUPERT	Schumann	86
LA PALOMA	Yradier	101
LAST ROSE OF SUMMER	Flotow	17
LARGO	Handel	81
LE COUCOU	Daquin	150
LONDONDERRY AIR	Irish Melody	60
LONG, LONG AGO	Bayly	12
LOVE'S OLD SWEET SONG	Molloy	31
MAZURKA IN B FLAT	Chopin	126
MELODY	Schumann	7
MELODY IN F	Rubinstein	28
MERRY WIDOW WALTZ	Lehar	134
MINUET (DON JUAN)	Mozart	15
MINUET IN G	Beethoven	100
MOMENT MUSICAL	Schubert	92
MUSETTE	Bach	27
OBERON	Von Weber	20
OLD BLACK JOE	Foster	117
ON THE MEADOW	Lichner	97
PEASANT DANCE	Baumfelder	36
PRELUDE No. 1 in C	Bach	148
PRELUDE OP. 28 No. 7	Chopin	95
PRELUDE OP. 28 No. 20	Chopin	95
ROMANCE	Schumann	107
SCARF DANCE	Chaminade	141
SERENADE	Schubert	132
SILENT NIGHT	Gruber	12
SOLDIERS' MARCH	Schumann	38
SONATINA	Clementi	30
SONG OF INDIA	Rimsky-Korsakoff	144
SPINNING SONG	Ellmenreich	90
SPRING SONG	Mendelssohn	64
STAR SPANGLED BANNER	Smith	63
SWAN, THE	Saint-Saens	70
SWANEE RIVER	Foster	116
TARANTELLA	Pieczonka	173
TRAUMEREI	Schumann	106
TRUMPETER'S SERENADE	Spindler	46
TULIP	Lichner	43
TURKEY IN THE STRAW	American Folk Song	22
TURKISH MARCH	Beethoven	14
UNFINISHED SYMPHONY	Schubert	34
VALSE BLEUE	Margis	128
VALSE LENTE (Coppelia)	Delibes	109
VENETIAN BOAT SONG No. 2	Mendelssohn	124
VIENNESE MELODY		62
VOICE OF THE HEART	van Gael	48
VOLGA BOAT SONG	Russian Folk Melody	78
WALTZ OP. 39	Tschaikowsky	54
WALTZ OF THE FLOWERS (Nutcracker Suite)	Tschaikowsky	113
WALTZ IN A FLAT	Brahms	122
WALTZING DOLL	Poldini	168

Grade I

French Child's Song

Franz Behr
(1837-1898)

Andantino

Grade I

In May

Franz Behr
(1837-1898)

Allegretto

Ah! Vous dirais-je maman

French Folk Tune

Grade I

Au Clair de la lune

French Folk Tune

"Surprise" Symphony
Theme from Andante

Grade I

Joseph Haydn
(1732-1809)

Melody
Op. 68

Grade I

Robert Schumann
(1810 - 1856)

Grade I

The Harebell

William Smallwood
(1831-1897)

Grade I

The Fair

Cornelius Gurlitt
(1820-1901)

Long, Long Ago

Grade I

Thomas Haynes Bayly
(1797- 1839)

Silent Night, Holy Night

Grade I

Franz Gruber
(1787 - 1863)

Grade II

Dark Eyes

Russian Folk Melody

Turkish March

(from "The Ruins Of Athens")

Grade II

Ludwig van Beethoven
(1770 - 1827)

Grade II

Minuet
(from "Don Juan")

Wolfgang Amadeus Mozart
(1756 - 1791)

Home Sweet Home

Grade II

Henry Rowley Bishop
(1786-1855)

Grade II

Last Rose of Summer

Friedrich von Flotow
(1812-1883)

Larghetto

Grade II

Gavotte in D

Johann Sebastian Bach
(1685-1750)

Grade II

Cradle Song

Carl Maria von Weber
(1786-1826)

Andante

p dolce e cantabile

dim. e rit.

pp

Grade II

Auld Lang Syne

Scotch Folk Song

Moderato

mf

dim. e poco rit.

Grade II

Cradle Song

Johannes Brahms
(1833-1897)

Theme
(from "Oberon")

Grade II

Carl Maria von Weber
(1786-1826)

Grade II

Turkey In The Straw

American Folk Tune

Grade II

Joyous Farmer

Robert Schumann
(1810-1856)

Allegro (*animato*)

Grade II

Avalanche

Stephen Heller
(1813-1888)

Allegro vivace

Grade II

Italian Song
Op. 39, No. 15

Peter I. Tschaikowsky,
(1840-1893)

Grade II

Musette

Johann Sebastian Bach
(1685-1750)

Grade II

Melody in F

Anton Rubinstein
(1829-1894)

In The Gloaming

Grade II

Annie F. Harrison

Andantino

Grade II

Sonatina
Op. 36, No. 1
(First Movement)

Muzio Clementi
(1752-1832)

Grade II

Love's Old Sweet Song

James Lyman Molloy
(1937-1909)

Grade II

Little Fairy Waltz

Op. 105, No. 1

Ludovic Streabbog,
(1835-1886)

Grade II

The Unfinished Symphony

(theme)

Franz Schubert
(1797-1828)

German Song

Grade II

Peter Tschaikowsky
(1840-1903)

Tranquillo

Grade II

Peasant Dance
Op. 208, No. 5

Friedrich Baumfelder
(1836-1916)

Allegretto

38

Grade II

Soldiers' March

Robert Schumann
(1810-1856)

Arabesque

Grade II

Johann Friedrich Burgmüller
(1806-1874)

Grade II

Waltz
(from "Faust")

Charles Gounod
(1818-1893)

Fine.

cresc.

rit.

D.C.

Funeral March

Grade II

Frédéric Chopin
(1810-1849)

Grade II

Tulip

Op. 111, No. 4

Heinrich Lichner
(1823-1898)

Allegretto

Trumpeter's Serenade

Grade II

Fritz Spindler
(1817-1905)

Grade II

The Voice Of The Heart
Op. 51

Henri Van Gael

Moderato e cantando

Grade II

At Home
Op. 134, No. 6

Heinrich Lichner
(1829-1898)

Allegro moderato

D.S. al Fine
poi la Trio

Trio

D.S. 𝄋 al Fine
poi la Coda

Coda

Gertrude's Dream Waltz

Grade II

Ludwig van Beethoven
(1770-1827)

(*) Small hands may omit the octave span, and play the lower note of the octave only.

Waltz In E Flat

Grade II

Peter Tschaikowsky
(1840-1893)

Allegro moderato

Grade II

In Rank And File

Gustav Lange
(1830-1889)

Allegro moderato (Tempo di Marcia)

Grade II

Londonderry Air

Irish Melody

Grade II

Viennese Melody

Andantino

The Star Spangled Banner

Grade III

John Stafford Smith
(1750-1836)

America

Grade III

Henry Carey
(1687 - 1743)

Spring Song

Grade III

Felix Mendelssohn
(1809 - 1847)

Allegretto grazioso

Consolation
Op. 30, No. 3

Grade III

Felix Mendelssohn
(1809 - 1847)

Adagio non troppo (♩=58)

Doll's Dream

Grade III
Cradle Song.

Theodore Oesten
(1813 - 1870)

The doll sleeps.

The doll's dream.

The doll wakes.

The doll dances.
Allegretto moderato

The Swan

Grade III

Camille-Saint-Saens
(1835 - 1921)

Grade III

Berceuse
(from "Jocelyn")

Benjamin Godard
(1849-1895)

Andantino

72

Für Elise

Grade III

Ludwig van Beethoven
(1770 - 1827)

Curious Story

Stephen Heller
(1813 - 1888)

Grade III

Volga Boat Song

Grade III

Russian Folk Melody

Angel's Serenade

Gaetano Braga
(1829-1907)

Grade III

Grade III

Largo

George Frederic Händel
(1685 - 1759)

Gavotte In G

Johann Sebastian Bach
(1685 - 1750)

Grade III

Allegro vivace

The Fountain
Op. 221

Grade III

Karl Bohm
(1844-1920)

Allegretto

Knight Rupert

Grade III

Robert Schumann
(1810 - 1856)

Allegro (♩ = 112)

Barcarolle
(from "Tales of Hoffmann")

Grade III

Jacques Offenbach
(1819 - 1880)

Spinning Song

Grade III

Albert Ellmenreich
(1816 - 1905)

Moment Musical

Grade III

Franz Schubert
(1797-1828)

Allegro moderato

Grade III

Gavotte

Johann Sebastian Bach
(1685-1750)

Moderato

Prelude
Op. 28, No. 7

Grade III

Frédéric Chopin
(1810-1849)

Prelude
Op. 28, No. 20

Grade III

Frédéric Chopin

Grade III

Album Leaf

Edvard Grieg
(1843-1907)

Allegretto

Grade III

On The Meadow
Op. 92, No. 5

Heinrich Lichner
(1829-1898)

Minuet In G

Grade III

Ludwig van Beethoven
(1770-1827)

Allegretto (ma non troppo)

legato con grazia

Fine

Trio

D.S. 𝄋 al Fine

La Paloma

Sebastien Yradier
(1809-1865)

Grandmother's Minuet
Op. 68, No. 2

Grade III

Edvard Grieg
(1843-1907)

Allegretto grazioso e leggierissimo

Grade III

Träumerei

Robert Schumann
(1810-1856)

Moderato (♩=100)

Grade III

Romanze
Op. 68, No. 19

Robert Schumann
(1810-1856)

Più moto ♩ = 130

Hungarian Dance No.5

Grade III

Johannes Brahms
(1833-1897)

Grade III

Valse Lente
(from the ballet "Coppélia")

Leo Delibes
(1836-1891)

Tempo di Valse

112

Grade III

Andante

Ludwig van Beethoven
(1770-1827)

Grade III

Waltz Of The Flowers
(from the "Nutcracker Ballet")

Peter Tschaikowsky
(1840-1893)

Tempo di Valse

Three American Folk Songs

I. Swanee River

Grade III

Stephen Foster
(1826-1864)

II. Kentucky Home

III. Old Black Joe

Grade III

Gipsy Dance

Heinrich Lichner
(1829-1898)

Allegro agitato

Grade III

Waltz in A Flat
Op. 39, No. 15

Johannes Brahms
(1833-1897)

Teneramente e grazioso (♩=116)

Venetian Boat Song
No. 2 (Op.30, No.6)

Grade III

Felix Mendelssohn
(1809-1847)

Allegretto tranquillo

Mazurka in B Flat

Op. 7, No. 1

Grade III

Frédéric Chopin
(1810-1849)

Valse Bleue

Grade III

Alfred Margis

marcato il canto

D.S.

Serenade

Franz Schubert
(1797-1828)

Grade III

Moderato

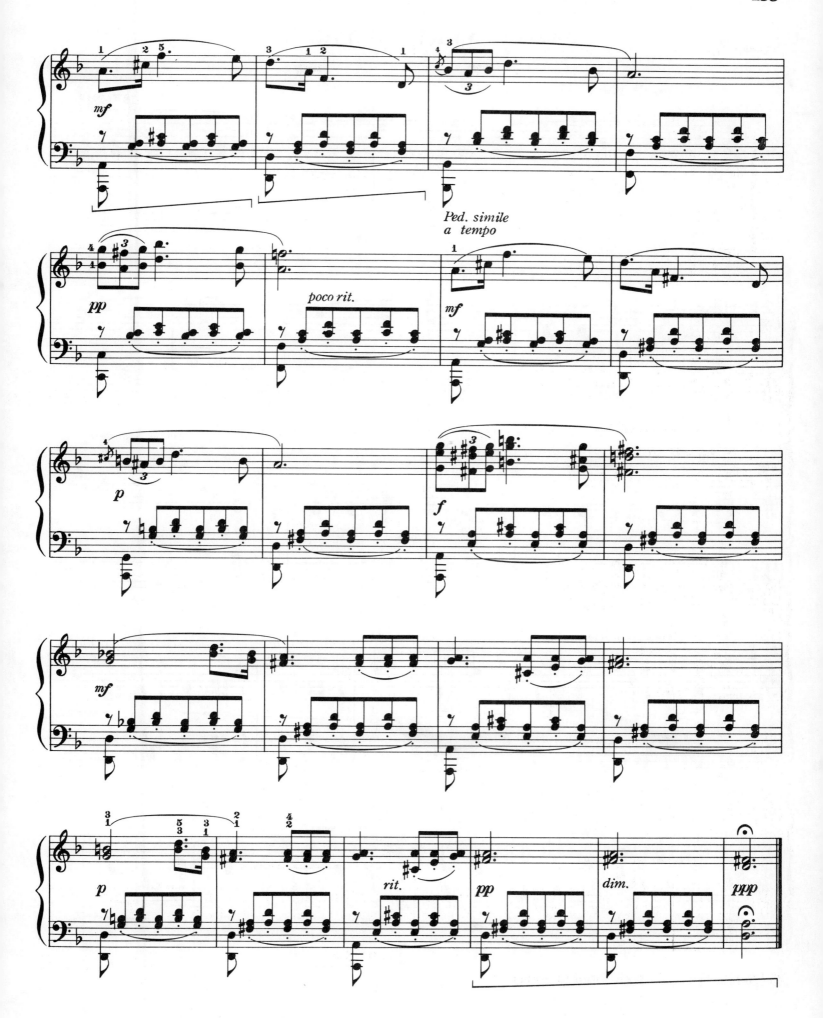

Merry Widow Waltz

Grade III

Franz Lehár
(1870-1948)

Tempo di Valse *Molto e tranquillo*

Camp Of The Gypsies

Op. 424, No. 3

Grade III

Franz Behr
(1837-1898)

Grade IV

Scarf - Dance

Cécil Chaminade
(1857-1944)

Song Of India

Grade IV

Nikolay Rimsky - Korsakov
(1844-1908)

Grade IV

Prelude
No. 1, from Well-tempered Clavichord

Johann Sebastian Bach
(1685-1750)

Le Coucou

Grade IV

Louis - Claude Daquin
(1694 - 1772)

Grade IV

Elegie
(Melodie Op. 10)

Jules Massenet
(1842-1912)

Lento, ma non troppo

Grade IV

Aragonaise

(from "Le Cid")

Jules Massenet
(1842-1912)

Assai vivo

Grade IV

Humoreske
Op. 101, No.7

Anton Dvořák
(1841-1904)

Poco lento e grazioso (♩ =72)

Chaconne

Grade IV

Auguste Durand
(1830-1909)

Allegretto

Waltzing Doll
Poupée Valsante

Grade IV

Eduard Poldini
(1869 - 1957)

Tempo di Valse

Grade IV

Tarantella

A. Pieczonka

Ecossaises

Grade IV

Ludwig van Beethoven - Busoni

Leggero ed animato

182

Grade IV

The Beautiful Blue Danube

Johann Strauss Jr.
(1825-1899)

Tempo di Valse

Piano Pieces for Children

INDEX BY GRADE — TEACHER'S GUIDE

GRADE I

AH! VOUS DIRAIS-JE-MAMAN	*French Folk Tune*	6
ANDANTE (*Surprise Symphony*)	*Haydn*	7
AU CLAIR DE LA LUNE	*French Folk Tune*	6
FAIR, THE	*Gurlitt*	10
FRENCH CHILD'S SONG	*Behr*	4
HAREBELL, THE	*Smallwood*	8
IN MAY	*Behr*	5
LONG, LONG AGO	*Bayly*	12
MELODY	*Schumann*	7
SILENT NIGHT	*Gruber*	12

GRADE II

ARABESQUE	*Burgmuller*	39
AT HOME	*Lichner*	50
AULD LANG SYNE	*Scotch Folk Tune*	19
AVALANCHE	*Heller*	24
CRADLE SONG	*Brahms*	20
CRADLE SONG	*Von Weber*	19
DARK EYES	*Russian Folk Song*	13
FAIRY WALTZ	*Streabogg*	32
FAUST WALTZ	*Gounod*	40
FUNERAL MARCH	*Chopin*	42
GAVOTTE IN D	*Bach*	18
GERMAN SONG	*Tschaikowsky*	35
GERTRUDE'S DREAM WALTZ	*Beethoven*	52
HOME SWEET HOME	*Bishop*	16
IN THE GLOAMING	*Harrison*	29
IN RANK AND FILE	*Lange*	56
ITALIAN SONG	*Tschaikowsky*	26
JOYOUS FARMER	*Schumann*	23
LAST ROSE OF SUMMER	*Flotow*	17
LOVE'S OLD SWEET SONG	*Molloy*	31
MELODY IN F	*Rubinstein*	28
MINUET (DON JUAN)	*Mozart*	15
MUSETTE	*Bach*	27
OBERON	*Von Weber*	20
PEASANT DANCE	*Baumfelder*	36
SOLDIERS' MARCH	*Schumann*	38
SONATINA	*Clementi*	30
TRUMPETER'S SERENADE	*Spindler*	46
TULIP	*Lichner*	43
TURKEY IN THE STRAW	*American Folk Song*	22
TURKISH MARCH	*Beethoven*	14
UNFINISHED SYMPHONY	*Schubert*	34
VOICE OF THE HEART	*van Gael*	48
WALTZ OP. 39	*Tschaikowsky*	54

GRADE III

AMERICA	*Carey*	63
ALBUMLEAF	*Grieg*	96
ANDANTE	*Beethoven*	112
ANGEL'S SERENADE	*Braga*	79
BARCAROLLE (*Tales of Hoffman*)	*Offenbach*	88
BERCEUSE (*Jocelyn*)	*Godard*	71
CAMP OF THE GYPSIES	*Behr*	136
CONSOLATION	*Mendelssohn*	66
CURIOUS STORY	*Heller*	76
DOLL'S DREAM	*Oesten*	67
FOUNTAIN, THE	*Bohm*	83
FUR ELISE	*Beethoven*	73
GAVOTTE	*Bach*	94
GAVOTTE IN G	*Bach*	82
GIPSY DANCE	*Lichner*	118
GRANDMOTHER'S MINUET	*Grieg*	104
HUNGARIAN DANCE	*Kleinmichel*	108
KENTUCKY HOME	*Foster*	116
KNIGHT RUPERT	*Schumann*	86
I A PALOMA	*Yradier*	101
LARGO	*Handel*	81
LONDONDERRY AIR	*Irish Melody*	60
MAZURKA IN B FLAT	*Chopin*	126
MERRY WIDOW WALTZ	*Lehar*	134
MINUET IN G	*Beethoven*	100
MOMENT MUSICAL	*Schubert*	92
OLD BLACK JOE	*Foster*	117
ON THE MEADOW	*Lichner*	97
PRELUDE OP. 28 No. 7	*Chopin*	95
PRELUDE OP. 28 No. 20	*Chopin*	95
ROMANCE	*Schumann*	107
SERENADE	*Schubert*	132
SPINNING SONG	*Ellemenreich*	90
SPRING SONG	*Mendelssohn*	64
STAR SPANGLED BANNER	*Smith*	63
SWAN, THE	*Saint-Saens*	70
SWANEE RIVER	*Foster*	116
TRAUMEREI	*Schumann*	106
VALSE BLEUE	*Margis*	128
VALSE LENTE (*Coppelia*)	*Delibes*	109
VENETIAN BOAT SONG No. 2	*Mendelssohn*	124
VIENNESE MELODY		62
VOLGA BOAT SONG	*Russian Folk Melody*	78
WALTZ IN A FLAT	*Brahms*	122
WALTZ OF THE FLOWERS (*Nutcracker Suite*)	*Tschaikowsky*	113

GRADE IV

ARAGONAISE	*Massenet*	156
BEAUTIFUL BLUE DANUBE	*Strauss*	186
CHACONNE	*Durand*	164
ECOSSAISES	*Beethoven-Busoni*	180
ELEGIE	*Massenet*	154
HUMORESQUE	*Dvorak*	160
LE COUCOU	*Daquin*	150
PRELUDE No. 1 in C	*Bach*	148
SCARF DANCE	*Chaminade*	141
SONG OF INDIA	*Rimsky-Korsakoff*	144
TARANTELLA	*Pieczonka*	173
WALTZING DOLL	*Poldini*	163